Optometrist

Written by John Parsons

Rigby

Chapter Snapshots

"Visiting an optometrist is fun,

3. Testing Equipment Page 16

Kate uses equipment to look inside
people's eyes. She also finds lenses
to make their eyesight perfect.

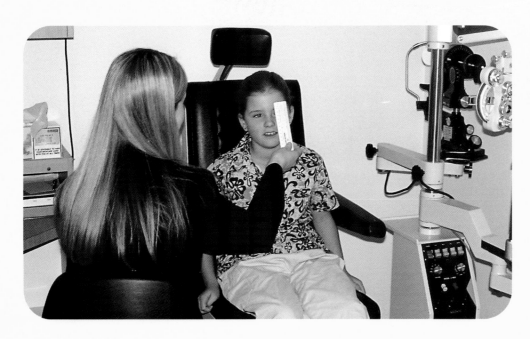

4. I Can See! Page 28

Now for the fun part! Kate has hundreds
of glasses to choose from. Which ones
would you choose?

because nothing ever hurts!"

Introduction

Meet Kate! Kate is 25 years old. During her free time, she enjoys going out with her friends, going to see new movies, and going to the gym.

Kate enjoys her working time, too. She has a very interesting job, looking after people's eyes. Kate is an optometrist.

What Does 'Optometrist' Mean?

Optometrist comes from two Greek words: *optos*, which means "to see," and *meter*, which means "to measure." An optometrist means "someone who measures what we see."

1. An Optometrist's Job

After finishing school, Kate had to decide what job she wanted to do. She knew that she wanted to have a job helping people.

At school, Kate had been good at math and science. So she decided to find a job where she could use math and science and help people, too.

When her parents suggested that she might want to be an optometrist, Kate knew that was a great idea!

For four years, Kate studied optometry at a university. Kate studied a lot of information about our eyes. She learned about the things that can go wrong with our eyes, and how our sight can be improved.

Kate learned how to test people's sight. If their sight was not good, Kate learned how to improve it.

A Baby's Eyesight

Newborn babies are unable to focus on things that are very close to them. Some babies look first with one eye and then the other. At about 4–5 months old, they use both eyes together! Up to the age of 5–6 months old, their eyesight keeps improving.

Look Inside

Pupil

The pupil is the opening through which light passes into the eye. It becomes larger in dim light and smaller in bright light.

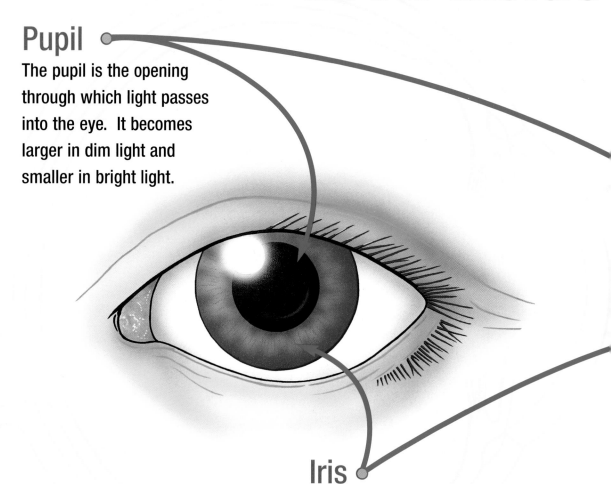

Iris

The iris is the colored part of the eye. Irises are usually brown, green, or blue. When it is dark, the iris opens wider to let more light through. When the light is very bright, the iris gets smaller to stop too much light from getting into the eye.

the Eye

Lens

The lens is the clear, curved part of the eye that focuses light onto the retina.

Retina

The retina contains special cells that can sense light and color.

Cornea

The cornea is the clear outer covering of the eye that light passes through first.

Tears

Tears are made in tear glands just above the eyes. Every time we blink, our eyelids spread tears over our eyes. This helps to keep them clean all the time.

2. A Visit to the Optometrist

Kate has been working as an optometrist for four years. People tell Kate that visiting an optometrist is fun, because nothing ever hurts! Kate likes to greet every person in a friendly way. It makes them feel relaxed.

Today, Kate will do many tests to check Charlotte's eyes and her sight.

Kate greets Charlotte.

10

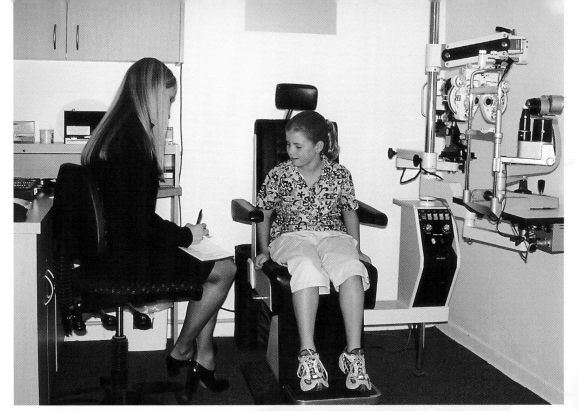

Charlotte sits in a special chair, while Kate writes notes about her eyes.

Kate starts by asking Charlotte if she has any problems with her sight.

Kate writes careful notes. If Charlotte comes back again, Kate's notes will remind her about what happened.

Family Eyesight Problems

An optometrist will ask patients if anyone else in their family has eyesight problems. Sometimes, sight problems can be passed on from parents to their children.

Kate washes her hands. She works with many people during the day, so Kate is careful about cleanliness.

Did You Know?

About 2 out of 10 children aged 6–16 need to wear glasses.

Age: 6–16

About 5 out of 10 adults aged 30–40 need to wear glasses.

Age: 30–40

About 9 out of 10 adults aged over 60 need to wear glasses.

Age: Over 60

Kate starts testing Charlotte's sight. She begins by asking her to read lines of letters on the letter chart.

F N P R Z

E Z H P V

D P N F R

R D F U V

U R Z V H

H N D R U

V P H D E

PVEHR

EHVDF

NUZFE

UHNZR

DNEFP

PUEPZ

Kate explains the letter chart to Charlotte.

Kate tests one eye at a time by covering the other eye with a piece of cardboard. Sometimes one eye can have better sight than the other. If Charlotte cannot read any letters, or lines of letters, Kate will write this in her notes.

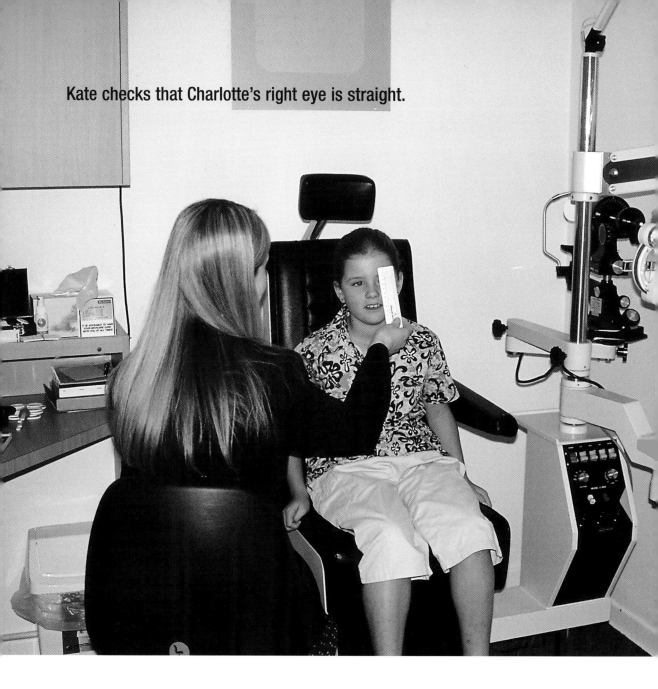

Kate checks that Charlotte's right eye is straight.

The next test checks that Charlotte's eyes are straight. Kate covers Charlotte's left eye and asks her to look in different directions. Then she checks Charlotte's right eye in the same way.

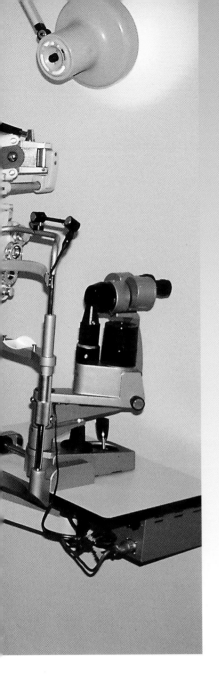

Eye Exercises

If a patient's eyes do not move properly, an optometrist can suggest some eye exercises. The exercises can help strengthen the muscles that move the eyes.

One exercise involves moving the eyes in different directions over and over again. Another exercise is to focus on something from different distances.

If the eye exercises do not help, a special eye doctor, called an ophthalmologist, may help the patient.

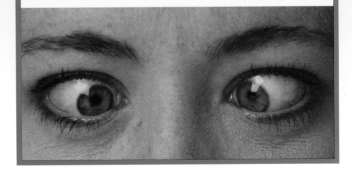

Next, Kate checks that Charlotte's eyes move properly. Kate slowly moves a pen around in front of Charlotte's face. Charlotte's eyes should follow the pen smoothly, as Kate moves it.

3. Testing Equipment

Kate uses special equipment to check the health of Charlotte's eyes and to test her sight.

A retinoscope will help Kate check the shape of the inside of Charlotte's eyes. A retinoscope is like a flashlight that shines a very thin line of light.

Lens Shape

If the lens in an eye is the wrong shape, it will not be able to focus clearly. Things may look blurry.

Kate shines the retinoscope into Charlotte's eyes. Its thin line of light will tell Kate if Charlotte is farsighted or nearsighted.

Farsighted People

Farsighted people can see things that are a long distance away quite clearly. They have problems clearly seeing things that are only a short distance away.

Nearsighted People

Nearsighted people can clearly see things that are a short distance away. They cannot clearly see things that are a long distance away.

Charlotte looks through different lenses in the lens machine.

Kate then uses a piece of equipment called the lens machine. It makes you look like you're in a science fiction movie! The lens machine allows Kate to quickly swap different lenses in front of Charlotte's eyes.

The lenses can make Charlotte's sight better or worse. Kate will find the best lenses to help Charlotte see perfectly with each eye.

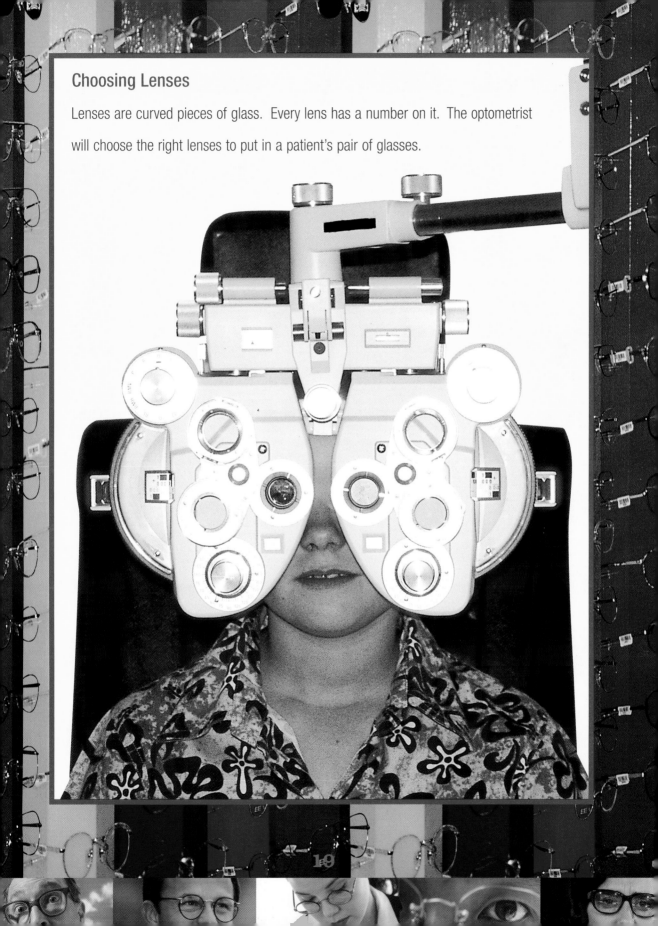

Choosing Lenses

Lenses are curved pieces of glass. Every lens has a number on it. The optometrist will choose the right lenses to put in a patient's pair of glasses.

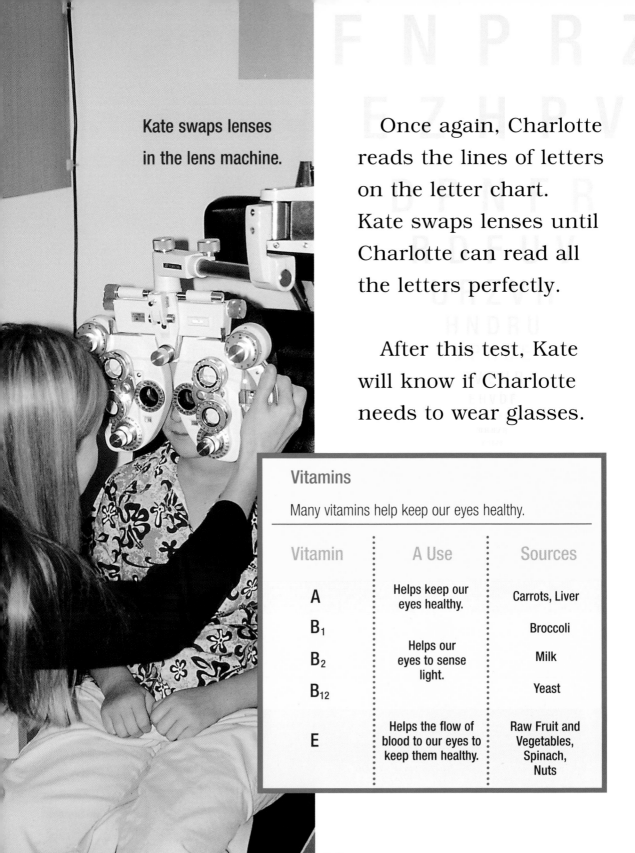

Kate swaps lenses in the lens machine.

Once again, Charlotte reads the lines of letters on the letter chart. Kate swaps lenses until Charlotte can read all the letters perfectly.

After this test, Kate will know if Charlotte needs to wear glasses.

Vitamins

Many vitamins help keep our eyes healthy.

Vitamin	A Use	Sources
A	Helps keep our eyes healthy.	Carrots, Liver
B_1		Broccoli
B_2	Helps our eyes to sense light.	Milk
B_{12}		Yeast
E	Helps the flow of blood to our eyes to keep them healthy.	Raw Fruit and Vegetables, Spinach, Nuts

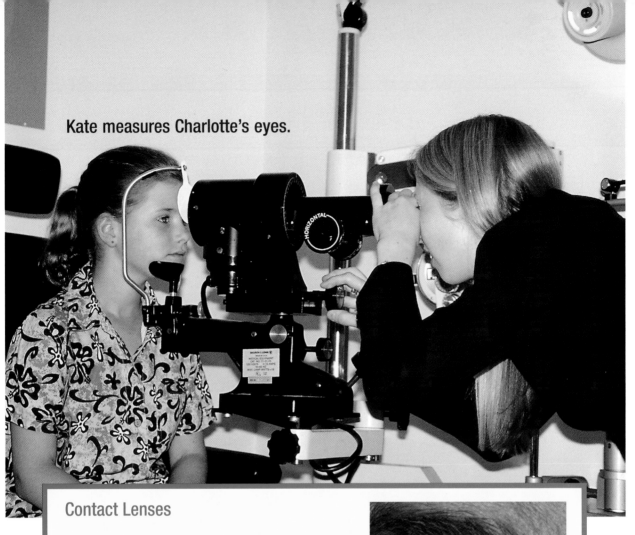

Kate measures Charlotte's eyes.

Contact Lenses

Patients can wear contact lenses instead of glasses. Contact lenses are thin, round pieces of soft plastic that sit on the surface of the eye.

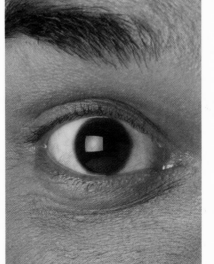

Contact lenses must be the right shape to feel comfortable and help a patient's sight. To measure the shape of a patient's eyes, the optometrist uses a piece of equipment called a keratometer.

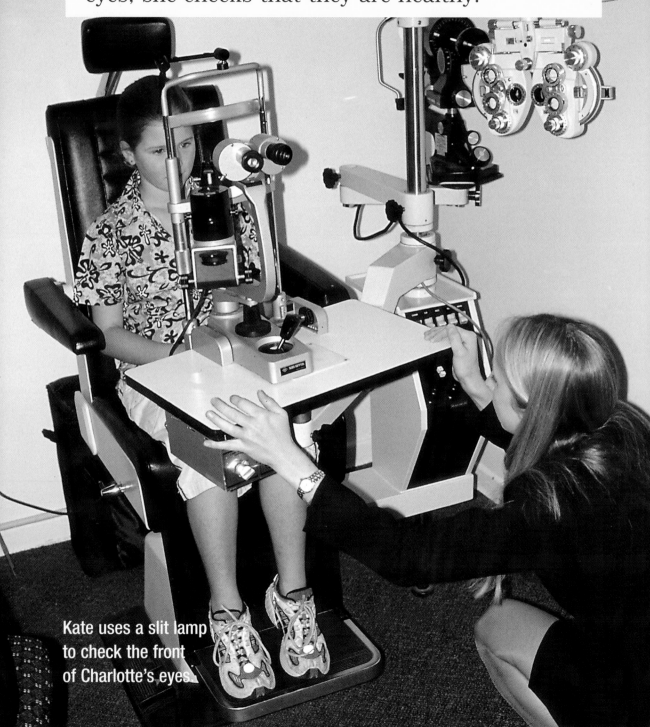

Eyes can get diseases, just like any other part of the body. When Kate is examining Charlotte's eyes, she checks that they are healthy.

Kate uses a slit lamp to check the front of Charlotte's eyes.

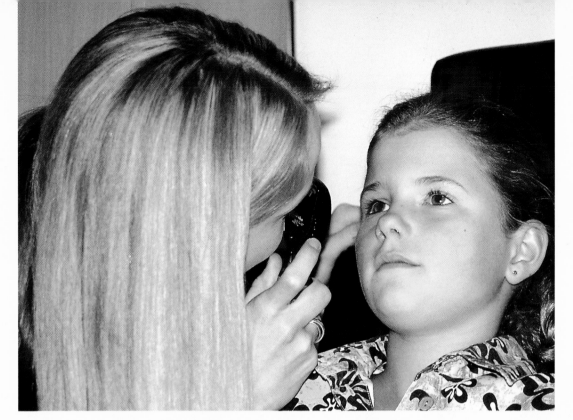

Kate uses an ophthalmoscope to check the back of Charlotte's eyes.

Kate needs to check the health of two parts in each eye: the front part and the back part. She uses a piece of equipment called a slit lamp to look at the front part of the eye. The slit lamp helps Kate to check if the iris, cornea, and the lens are healthy.

Kate uses an ophthalmoscope to check the back part of the eye. The ophthalmoscope is a special flashlight with a magnifying glass. Kate looks through it to check the retina and the blood vessels in the back of the eye.

There are many other tests that Kate can ask Charlotte to do. She will do three more tests.

The first test is a binocular test. In this test, Kate can check if Charlotte is able to judge distances properly. For the second test, Kate asks Charlotte to wear special 3-D glasses to check if she can see objects as the right shape.

Charlotte wears 3-D glasses.

Why Do We Have Two Eyes?

We have two eyes to help us judge distance and depth. When two eyes work together, it is called binocular vision.

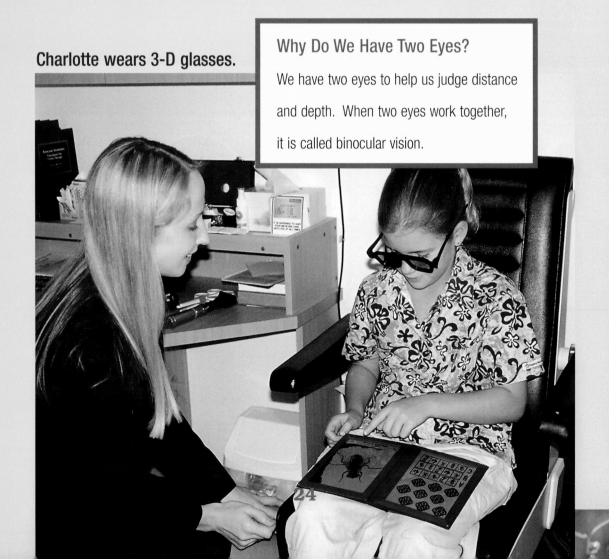

Charlotte does the color-sight test.

A Color Test

If you have perfect
color vision, you
could read this:

If you do not have
perfect color
vision, the words
might look gray.

If Kate was testing the eyes of a boy or a man, she might test whether he can see colors properly. Some boys and men cannot tell the difference between some colors, such as red and green. Charlotte can see colors perfectly, but she wants to do this last test just for fun!

Optometry Time Line

In the year...
100

The Romans used clear jars of water to help them read better.

In the year...
1268

Flat-bottomed lenses, called reading stones, were used in England.

In the year...
1300

The first glasses were invented in Italy, for farsighted people.

In the year…

1500

Glasses for nearsighted people were invented.

In the year…

1784

Bifocal glasses, for farsighted and nearsighted people were invented.

In the year…

1930

Plastic contact lenses were invented for farsighted and nearsighted people.

4. I Can See!

Kate has finished testing Charlotte's sight and the health of her eyes. All the tests show that Charlotte has perfect sight.

However, some people do not have perfect sight. They may choose to wear glasses to help them see better. Kate has many styles of glasses so patients can choose a pair that they like!

Charlotte enjoys trying on some of the glasses, just for fun!